The

Senior's Guide
to Computer Tips and Tricks

Windows XP®, Internet Explorer®,
Microsoft® Word, and Outlook®

The

Senior's Guide
to Computer Tips and Tricks

Windows XP®, Internet Explorer®, Microsoft® Word, and Outlook®

By Rebecca Sharp Colmer,
and
Todd M. Thomas

EKLEKTIKA PRESS
Chelsea, Michigan

Table of Contents

Table of Contents

Table of Contents

Table of Contents

Table of Contents

Table of Contents

Table of Contents

Disclaimer

Every effort has been made to make this book as complete as possible and as accurate as possible. However, there may be mistakes both typographical and in content. Therefore, this text should be used as a general guide and not the ultimate source of information.

LIMIT OF LIABILITY/DISCLAIMER OF WARRANTY: THE PUBLISHER AND THE AUTHORS MAKE NO REPRESENTATIONS OR WARRANTIES WITH RESPECT TO THE ACCURACY OR COMPLETENESS OF THE CONTENTS OF THIS WORK AND SPECIFICALLY DISCLAIM ALL WARRANTIES, INCLUDING WITHOUT LIMITATION WARRANTIES OF FITNESS FOR A PARTICULAR PURPOSE. NO WARRANTY MAY BE CREATED OR EXTENDED BY SALES OR PROMOTIONAL MATERIALS. THE ADVICE AND STRATEGIES CONTAINED HEREIN MAY NOT BE SUITABLE FOR EVERY SITUATION. THIS WORK IS SOLD WITH THE UNDERSTANDING THAT THE PUBLISHER IS NOT ENGAGED IN RENDERING LEGAL, ACCOUNTING, OR OTHER PROFESSIONAL SERVICES. IF PROFESSIONAL ASSISTANCE IS REQUIRED, THE SERVICES OF A COMPETENT PROFESSIONAL PERSON SHOULD BE SOUGHT. NEITHER THE PUBLISHER NOR THE AUTHORS SHALL BE LIABLE FOR DAMAGES ARISING HEREFROM. THE FACT THAT AN ORGANIZATION OR WEBSITE IS REFERRED TO IN THIS WORK AS A CITATION AND/OR POTENTIAL SOURCE OF FURTHER INFORMATION DOES NOT MEAN THAT THE AUTHORS OR THE PUBLISHER ENDORSES THE INFORMATION THE ORGANIZATION OR WEBSITE MAY PROVIDE OR RECOMMENDATIONS IT MAY MAKE. FURTHER, READERS SHOULD BE AWARE THAT INTERNET WEBSITES LISTED IN THIS WORK MAY HAVE CHANGED OR DISAPPEARED BETWEEN WHEN IT WAS WRITTEN AND WHEN IT IS READ. NEITHER THE PUBLISHER NOR AUTHORS SHALL BE LIABLE FOR ANY LOSS OF PROFIT OR ANY OTHER COMMERCIAL DAMAGES, INCLUDING BUT NOT LIMITED TO SPECIAL, INCIDENTAL, CONSEQUENTIAL, OR OTHER DAMAGES. THE AUTHORS AND PUBLISHER SPECIFICALLY DISCLAIM ANY LIABILITY, LOSS, OR RISK, PERSONAL OR OTHERWISE, WHICH IS INCURRED AS A CONSEQUENCE, DIRECTLY OR INDIRECTLY, OF THE USE AND APPLICATION OF ANY OF THE CONTENTS OF THIS BOOK.

Getting The Most From This Book

We wrote this book for people of all computer experience levels. We took care to write the tips as simply as we could. Nonetheless you still must have some computer experience to get the most from this book. You should be sitting at your computer and trying each tip as you read it.

To make the material easier to follow we tried to use certain styles to convey the instructions. Here is the formatting style we used:

- Buttons, window titles, list boxes, essentially all nouns, are in bold font. Ex. **OK**, **CANCEL**.
- Some tips are listed as bullets, like this list. These do not need to be followed in any order.
- Tips shown as a numbered list should be followed in the order listed.
- Never type the quotes listed as a command. Ex: "c:\dir", ignore the quotes "".
- When you must press two or more keys simultaneously we use the + symbol. CTRL+X means hold the "CTRL" button down while pressing the "X" button.
- Words such as Click, Choose, Select mean making a left-mouse click.

Introduction

Computers have made life so much easier for mankind. Many tasks that we used to do manually, which consumed many hours of our day, now are done in seconds with the use of a computer.

This book is a compilation of shortcuts and tips to help make using your computer even easier and faster. We all have gotten into habit patterns for computer usage. In this book, we will show you new ways to accomplish the tasks you already do as well as new things you can do.

PART 1

Windows XP Shortcuts and Tips

Windows XP is an operating system introduced in 2001 by Microsoft. The "XP" in Windows XP stands for "eXPerience."

Besides a revamped user interface, XP has improved support for gaming, digital photography, networking, and the Internet.

In this section, you will learn some tips and shortcuts related to the XP operating system, which range from creating custom screen savers to surfing the net!

Controlling The Control Panel

Windows XP gives you two views of the Control Panel application. The Control Panel allows you to configure and customize your operating system. It is a very important application and key to using a lot of tips in this book. So it is essential to be able to switch between the different views, Category and Classic.

Figure 1 shows the Control Panel in the Category View. This is the default. It groups items together that provide a similar function. Clicking on the **Switch to Classic View** line in the Task Bar (located on the left side of the Control Panel) changes the Control Panel to the Classic View.

The Classic View, see Figure 2, lists everything without categorizing them. If you want quick access to system control applications, then this is for you. You can switch back to the Category view by clicking on the **Switch to Category View** on the Task Bar.

Controlling The Control Panel, Cont.

Figure 1: Control panel in category view

Figure 2: Control panel in classic view

Access The Start Menu Using The Windows Key

Often it is quicker to type on your keyboard than to use the mouse. Moving your hand to and from the mouse wastes time. Using keyboard shortcuts can save you time.

A very simple keyboard shortcut you can use is the "Windows" key. It is located between the **CTRL** key and the **ALT** key on the LEFT side of the keyboard. Depending on the manufacturer of your keyboard, this key may be duplicated on the RIGHT side of the keyboard, just to the right of the **ALT** key.

Pressing the Windows key opens the Start Menu on the taskbar. You can then use the arrow keys to navigate the Start Menu or switch to the mouse after you press the key.

Use The Menu Key Instead
Of Right-Clicking

Besides the Windows key, most keyboards have a Menu key, which mimics a right-click on your mouse.

On most keyboards it is located on the right side of the keyboard between the Windows key and the **CTRL** key.

Give it a try:

1. Select **My Computer** on your desktop.
2. Press the **Menu** key on your keyboard. You will see a menu pop up, that is the same as if you right-clicked on **My Computer**.

Make Fonts Sharper Using ClearType

Do you think the fonts on your screen look fuzzy? With Windows XP you can greatly improve their clarity, especially if you are using a LCD (i.e., flat panel monitor). Microsoft's ClearType technology smooths all fonts at all sizes.

To enable ClearType:

1. Click **Start**, choose **Control Panel**, and then select **Appearance and Themes**.
2. Double-click the **Display** icon, then the **Appearance** tab, and then **Effects**.
3. Select **ClearType** from the list. Click under the **Use the following method to smooth edges of screen fonts** check box. See Figure 3.
4. Click **OK**, and then click **OK** again.

Your fonts should appear significantly sharper, smoother, and clearer.

Make Fonts Sharper Using ClearType, Cont.

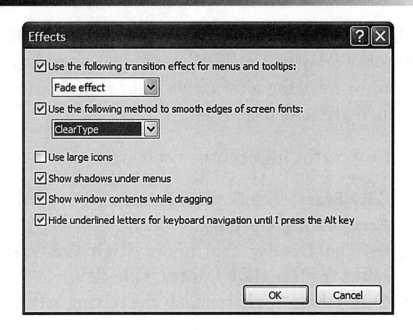

Figure 3: Effects dialog box

Use The High Contrast Screen Setting For Easier Reading

The high contrast setting makes it easier for people who have a vision impairment to read the monitor by using alternative color combinations to increase screen contrast.

To turn on the high contrast setting:

1. Click **Start**, click **Control Panel**, and then click **Accessibility Options**.
2. On the **Display** tab, under **High Contrast**, select the **Use High Contrast** check box.
3. Click **OK** or **Apply** to make the setting active.

To turn off High Contrast, clear the **Use High Contrast** check box.

Hide File Names In Thumbnail View

A thumbnail image is a small preview of a larger image that appears in a folder. It is similar to an icon. Thumbnails provide a great way to preview images without having to open them in an image editor or Microsoft Image Viewer.

However, thumbnails are larger than icons and therefore you cannot view as many files in a folder. Turning off the file names associated with the thumbnails may be the answer.

To turn off the file names display, hold down the **SHIFT** key when you open a folder or when you switch into Thumbnail view from another view such as List.

This will turn off the file names, giving more space for the thumbnails. Doing it again turns them back on.

How To Disable/Enable The Windows Firewall

The most current version of Windows XP Service Pack ships with a firewall enabled by default.

For example, you may want to turn it off to use a firewall bundled with your anti-virus software. Here is how to disable the firewall:

1. Click **Start** then choose **Control Panel**.
2. Double click **Security Center** then choose **Firewall**.
3. Click the **General** tab, then click the **Off** radio button. See Figure 4 on the next page.
4. After turning off the firewall, a balloon will popup in the system tray stating that a firewall isn't running. Click the **X** to close the balloon.

WARNING: We recommend that you run a firewall of some sort on your computer. If you turn off XP's firewall, make sure you have another one enabled.

Why, you ask? You're running a greater risk of getting a virus, spyware, and/or other hacker attacks if you don't run a firewall.

How To Disable/Enable The Windows Firewall, Cont.

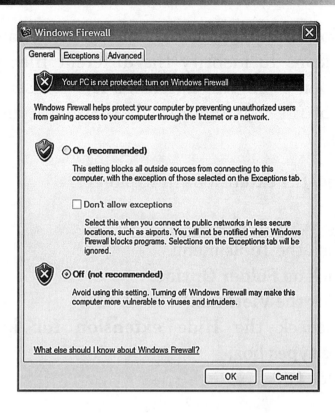

Figure 4: Firewall dialog box

View File Extensions In Explorer

Windows XP hides file extensions by default. It uses icons to identify the different file types. However, seeing the extension lets you see what type of file it is more easily than with an icon alone.

To view file extensions in Explorer:

1. Open any folder.
2. Click the **Tools** menu.
3. Click on **Folder Options**.
4. Click the **View** tab.
5. Uncheck the **Hide extension for known file types** box.
6. Click **OK**.

Now you should be able to see the extensions.

Stop A CD-ROM From
Automatically Starting

By default, when you place a CD-ROM into your computer, XP tries to run it. If it is an installation CD-ROM the setup program will start. If it is music, Windows Media Player launches.

However, if you only want to see the CD-ROM's content, you can temporarily disable this feature so nothing happens when you insert a CD-ROM.

Here's how:

1. Open your CD-ROM player as normal.
2. Place your CD into the CD-ROM tray.
3. Press the **SHIFT** key while simultaneously closing the CD-ROM tray.

That's it.

How To Disable Error Reporting

Although Windows XP is significantly more stable than previous versions of Windows, applications still crash.

When a program crashes, XP offers to send the error to Microsoft so they can troubleshoot the problem. If you do not want to do this, you can turn off error reporting.

Here are the steps:

1. Open the **Control Panel**.
2. Click on **Performance and Maintenance**.
3. Click on **System**.
4. Cick on the **Advanced** tab.
5. Click on the **Error-reporting** button at the bottom of the window.
6. Select **Disable error reporting**.
7. Click **OK**.
8. Click **OK**.

Even with the feature enabled you can still decline to have the error message sent to Microsoft.

How To Activate The Screen Saver
With A Shortcut

Add a shortcut to your desktop to start your screen saver with a double-click:

1. Click the **Start** button, and then click **Search**.
2. In the **Search Companion** window, click **All files and folders**.
3. In the **All or part of file name** box type "***.scr**" (without the quotes). See Figure 5 below.
4. In the **Look In** box, choose **Local Hard Drives (C:)** or the drive where you have system files stored on your computer.
5. Click **Search** to see a list of screen savers in the results. Pick the screen saver you want. You can preview it by double-clicking it.
6. Right click on the file, choose **Send To**, and then click **Desktop** (create shortcut).
7. To activate the screen saver, double-click the icon on your desktop.

**Figure 5: Search screen
for screen savers**

Group Files For Easier Management

You might find it hard to locate a particular file buried in a long list of file names in My Computer or Windows Explorer. Grouping files by their name, size, modified date, or type may make it easier to locate the one you are looking for.

To group files:

1. Open any **My Computer** or **Explorer** window.
2. Select **View**, choose **Arrange Icons by**. See Figure 6 below.
3. Click **Show in Groups**.
4. You can choose how to organize the files by selecting View and choosing Arrange Icons by selecting either name, size, modified date, or type.

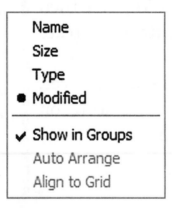

Figure 6: Show in groups menu

Switch The Start Menu Style

Does the new Windows XP Start menu confuse you? Are you used to the old-style menu? You can easily change to the Windows Classic Start Menu by following these steps:

1. Right-click the **Start** button, and then click **Properties**.
2. Click the **Classic Start menu**.
3. You can optionally click the **Customize** button to select items to display on the Start Menu.
4. Your Start Menu should look like a pre-Windows XP style.

Remove Unwanted Icons From Your Desktop

If you use the Classic Start menu, Windows XP also adds the My Documents, My Computer, My Network Places, and Internet Explorer icons to your desktop.

If you don't want these icons to appear, or you want fewer icons:

1. Right-click a blank area on the Desktop.
2. Choose **Properties**, and then navigate to the **Desktop** tab.
3. Click **Customize Desktop** to choose which icons you want on the desktop.
4. Click **OK**, then **OK** again.

Create A Screen Saver Slideshow

Why not create a screen saver slideshow on your monitor using your favorite images? It's a perfect way to display your digital photos or other images so others can see them.

Here's how to create a slideshow screen saver:

1. Right-click a blank area on your Desktop and click **Properties**.
2. Click the **Screen Saver** tab.
3. In the **Screen Saver** list, click **My Pictures Slideshow**.
4. Choose the directory where your images exist.
5. Click **Settings** to make any adjustments, such as how often the pictures should change, what size they should be, and whether you'll use transition effects between pictures.
6. Click **OK**.

Place Your Most Used Programs Near The Top Of The Start Menu

Do you have a favorite application that you frequently use? If so, you can place it at the top of the Start Menu for easier access. After all, it always helps to know where things are.

Here's how:

1. Right-click the link to your favorite program on the **Start Menu** and select **Pin to Start Menu**.
2. The program will be moved permanently to the top area of the list, just below your browser and e-mail programs.

Create A Shortcut On Your Desktop

You can quickly access programs and files by placing a shortcut icon to them on your desktop.

Here's how:

1. Right-click **Start**, and then click **Explore**.
2. Locate the folder, file, or program, and then click the item to open it.
3. Click the icon representing the item.
4. Click **File** on the toolbar, and then **Create Shortcut** on the drop-down menu that appears.
5. Right-click on the shortcut icon that is created.
6. Choose **Send To** from the drop-down menu, and then click **Desktop** (create shortcut) on the submenu that appears.

Choose A Windows Sound Scheme

Windows XP ships with a really nice sound scheme. However, it's not loaded by default for some reason. So once you've installed Windows XP, one of the first things you should do is load the new sound scheme.

To do so:

1. Open up **Control Panel** and navigate to **Sounds, and Audio Devices**.
2. Choose the tab titled **Change the Sounds scheme**. In the dialog that appears, choose **Windows Default** for the sound scheme. Windows will ask you whether you want to save the previous scheme. Since no scheme was previously loaded, choose **No**.
3. Click **APPLY**.
4. Click **OK** to exit the dialog.

The Senior's Guide to Computer Tips & Tricks

Work With Sound Effects Using Windows XP

Windows XP offers more than just visual customization. You can also customize its sound effects.

To add sound effects:

1. Click **Start**, then click **Control Panel**.
2. Click **Sounds, and Audio Devices**.
3. On the **Sounds** tab, under **Program** events, click the event to which you want to apply a sound.
4. In the **Sounds** list, click the sound you want to link to the event.
5. To hear the sound, click the **Play** button to the right of the **Sounds** list. When satisfied, click **OK**. Repeat steps 4 and 5 until you have linked sounds as you want.
6. Click **Save As** and type a name for the sound scheme, and then click **OK**.
7. Click **OK** to complete the procedure.

Create MP3 Files Using Windows Media Player

The relationship between Media Player for Windows XP (MPXP) and the MP3 audio format is widely misunderstood.

Windows Media Player is able to playback MP3 files out of the box. Copying CD audio into MP3 format will require an MP3 plug-in. In other words you cannot create MP3 files with Windows Media Player. It only creates Windows Media Audio (wma) formats.

Don't despair. To enable MP3 encoding in Windows XP, you can purchase a MP3 creation add-on pack for Windows XP.

Checkout www.microsoft.com/windowsmedia for a list of software vendors.

Add An Item To The Send To Menu

When you right-click on an item you will see the **Send To** menu. This menu allows you to send the item to a program, printer, or even e-mail it.

You can create a new shortcut on the **Send To** menu, for example, one that sends a file to a frequently-used folder. Here's how:

1. Open **My Computer**, and double-click the drive where Windows is installed, which is usually drive C.
2. Double-click the **Documents and Settings** folder, and then double-click the folder for a particular user, in this case it is probably your user name.
3. Double-click the **Send To** folder. The **Send To** folder is hidden by default. If it is hidden, click **Tools**, click **Folder Options**, and then click **Show hidden files and folders**.
4. On the **File** menu, point to **New**, and then click **Shortcut**.
5. Follow the instructions to create a shortcut to whatever application or folder you want to send the item to.

Now, when you right-click a file, and click **Send To**, the shortcut to the item you selected will be an option.

Alphabetize Your Menus

You might find it annoying that new programs and icons add themselves to the bottom of the Start Menu. This can make them hard to find. Fortunately you can alphabetize the Start Menu to make programs easier to find.

To arrange the items by name, follow these instructions:

1. Click **Start**, click **All Programs**, and then right-click on any folder or icon.
2. Click **Sort by Name**.

Place A Picture On A Folder

Use pictures, on a folder icon, to remind you of its contents, or just to make it more fun. Follow these steps to change the folder picture:

1. Right-click a folder, and then click **Properties**.
2. Click the **Customize** tab, and then click **Choose Picture**.
3. Select any image on your computer. (You may have to navigate to where the image is stored.) Click **Open**, and then click **OK**.

Here are some caveats to using a picture on a folder:

- If your folder doesn't contain an image file, Windows won't generate a folder picture.

- You can only see a picture on a folder when it's in **Thumbnails** view within another folder. To switch to **Thumbnails** view, on the **View** menu of the open folder, click **Thumbnails**.

How To Copy A File Or Folder Using The Task Pane

Windows XP's Task Pane makes it easy to copy a file from one folder to another. Here is how to copy a file using the Task Pane:

Navigate to the file you want to copy.

1. Click on the file or folder you want to copy.
2. In the **File and Folder Tasks** section, click **Copy this file** or **Copy this folder**. See Figure 7 on the next page for an example of the task bar showing these commands.
3. In **Copy Items**, select destination folder. If you scroll to the top of the folder list you'll see the **Desktop and My Documents**. If you need to copy the file to a sub-folder, simply click the + sign beside the folder to expand its contents.
4. Once you find, and click on, the destination, click **Copy**.

How To Move A File Or Folder Using The Task Pane

Moving a file with XP's Task Pane is similar to copying it. All you do is:

1. Click the file in the right-hand pane that you want to move.
2. Click **Move This File** in the Task Pane. See Figure 7. A **Move Items** dialog box will appear.
3. Use the **Move Items** dialog to locate the destination folder. Once you've found the destination folder and clicked it, click the **Move** button to complete the move.

Figure 7: Task Pane with Copy and Move Commands

How To Undelete Files

We've all been too quick on the **Delete** key and sent the wrong file or folder to the Recycle Bin.

Because you must explicitly empty the Recycle Bin before permanently removing the file, you have a good chance to undelete files. If you need to recover a file:

1. Double-click the **Recycle Bin** to open it.
2. Locate the file you wish to undelete.
3. Right-click the file you wish to undelete to display a pop-up menu and choose **Restore** to restore the file to its previous location.
4. Optionally, you can restore it to another location by dragging it onto the Desktop or into another folder.

Selecting Multiple Files

At some point you will need to select more than one file to copy, move, print, or delete. Here is how to select multiple files when that time occurs:

1. Hold down the **CTRL** key while you click each file you wish to select.
2. To deselect an already selected file, hold down the **CTRL** and click it.
3. To select a whole list of files or folders, click the top file in the list, hold down the **SHIFT** key and click the last file in the list.

Create A Shutdown Shortcut

You can create a desktop shortcut to quickly shutdown or restart your PC with this handy tip.

To create either of these handy shortcuts:

1. Right click an empty area of the Desktop or folder where you wish to create the shortcut.
2. Click **New** then **Shortcut**.
3. For the location of the shortcut, enter **shutdown -s -t 01** for a shutdown command or **shutdown -r -t 01** for a restart.
4. Click **Next** to and give your shortcut an appropriate name like **Shutdown** or **Restart**.
5. Click **Finish**.

Organize Your Desktop Icons

After a hard day of computing, you may find your desktop icons scattered everywhere. To easily rearrange and re-align them:

1. Right-click on an empty area of the desktop.
2. Choose **Arrange Icons By**.
3. Pick the Method to arrange them by either **Name**, **Size**, **Type**, or **Modified**.

Capture Screenshots In Windows XP

Windows XP ships with a screen-capture utility that is attached to the **PRINT SCREEN** key on your keyboard. This is a handy utility if you want to take a picture of all or part of your screen. The images in this book are screenshots.

Pressing the **PRINT SCREEN** key will capture the entire desktop to your clipboard, ready to be pasted into an application.

Pressing **ALT+PRINT SCREEN** will grab only the currently active window on the desktop.

To use these captured images, you will need to open an image-editing program like Adobe Photoshop or Microsoft Paint and paste the image into a new file using **CTRL+V**.

How To Find My IP Address

At some point you may need to know the IP address of your computer. This might happen if you are working with your Internet Service Provider troubleshooting a problem.

Finding your computer's IP address is straightforward:

1. Click the **Start** menu and click **Run**.
2. Type **cmd** in the box and click **OK**. Another window appears.
3. Type "**ipconfig /all**" without the quotes. Your IP address is on the line labeled **IP address...** in the listing. Figure 8 shows a computer with an IP address of 192.168.1.10.
4. Press **Enter**.

```
C:\WINDOWS\system32\cmd.exe                                        _ □ ×

C:\Documents and Settings>ipconfig /all

Windows IP Configuration

        Host Name . . . . . . . . . . . . : xp
        Primary Dns Suffix  . . . . . . . :
        Node Type . . . . . . . . . . . . : Unknown
        IP Routing Enabled. . . . . . . . : No
        WINS Proxy Enabled. . . . . . . . : No

Ethernet adapter Local Area Connection:

        Connection-specific DNS Suffix  . :
        Description . . . . . . . . . . . : 3Com 3C905TX-based Ethernet Adapter
(Generic)
        Physical Address. . . . . . . . . : 00-60-97-9C-37
        Dhcp Enabled. . . . . . . . . . . : No
        IP Address. . . . . . . . . . . . : 192.168.1.10
        Subnet Mask . . . . . . . . . . . : 255.255.255.0
        Default Gateway . . . . . . . . . : 192.168.1.1
        DNS Servers . . . . . . . . . . . : 192.168.1.1

C:\Documents and Settings>_
```

Figure 8: IP address listing with ipconfig

How To Always Win At Freecell

FreeCell is a game that ships with Windows XP. It is fun, challenging, and difficult to win. If you've never won, but desperately want to, try this trick:

At any time during the game do the following:

1. Type **CTRL+SHIFT+F10**.
2. A screen with three options will appear.
3. Choose **Abort** then make a play and you should win the game.

How To Cheat At Minesweeper

Ever won at Minesweeper? If not, don't feel bad, it's a tough game. So try this "cheat" that will reveal the mines as you play:

1. Start **Minesweeper**.
2. Type "xyzzy" (don't use quotes).
3. Hit **SHIFT** and **ENTER** at the same time.
4. Minimize all application windows that hide the desktop. The uppermost pixel in the top left corner of your desktop will turn black when your mouse is over a mine, and white when it's safe to click. The pixel is tough to see, but it is there.

This tip works best if you have a black desktop so the tiny white pixel is easy to see.

Disable File Indexing To Speed Up XP

Windows XP can improve its search speed by indexing your files. In essence, it pre-searches them.

The downside to improved searching speed is that your PC will be constantly indexing files as you use them. This process can bog down your computer. So if you don't use the search feature very often, here is how to disable file indexing:

1. Open **My Computer**.
2. Right click on one of your hard drive icons and then select **Properties**.
3. At the bottom of the window you should see **Allow indexing service to index this disk for faster searches** uncheck this and click, then click on **OK**. See Figure 9 for the location of this checkbox.
4. A new window will pop up and select **Apply to all folders and subfolders**. It takes a few seconds to apply the change to all the files and folders. The more items you have, the longer the process will take.

Disable File Indexing To Speed Up XP, Cont.

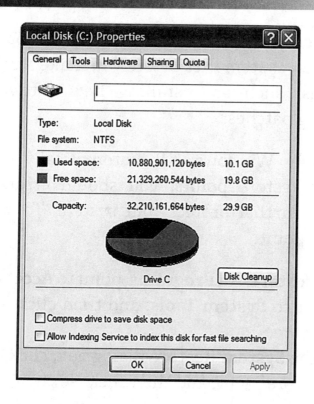

Figure 9: Local disk indexing option

Create Your Own System Restore Points

To protect your system you should take a "snapshot" of critical system files before you make any major changes, such as installing new software or applying patches.

Although Windows XP automatically creates system restore points, you should create your own to further protect your system. To create a restore point:

1. Click **Start**, **All Programs**, point to **Accessories**, point to **System Tools**, and then click **System Restore**.
2. In the **System Restore** dialog box, click **Create a restore point**, and then click **Next**.
3. Type a description for your restore point, such as "**Before Office XP**", then click **Create**.

If your system fails, press **F8** during the boot process, and then choose **Last known good configuration**. Windows XP boots your system to the most recent restore point.

How To Turn On ToggleKeys For Sound Cues

ToggleKeys are designed for people who have a vision impairment. When ToggleKeys are turned on, your computer provides sound cues when the locking keys (CAPS, NUM, or SCROLL LOCK) are pressed. A high sound plays when the keys are switched on and a low sound plays when they are switched off.

Here is the procedure to enable ToggleKeys:

1. Click **Start**, click **Control Panel**, and then click **Classic View** in the **Task Pane**.
2. Double-click the **Accessibilities Options** icon.
3. Click the **Keyboard** tab.
4. Under **ToggleKeys**, select the **Use ToggleKeys** check box.
5. Click **Settings** then select the **Use shortcut** check box to use the keyboard shortcut by pressing the **NUM LOCK** key for five seconds.
6. Click **APPLY**, then **OK**.

Enable Auto-Logon To Windows XP

You can configure Windows XP to automatically log on for you. Enabling auto-logon makes your computer more convenient to use, but can pose a security risk. It allows others to access your computer without your knowledge.

However, if you want the convenience of auto log on, here is how to enable it:

1. Click **Start**, click **Run**, and type **control userpasswords2**.
2. Clear the **Users must enter a username and password to use this computer** check box.
3. Click **Apply** to open another dialog box.
4. Enter the user name and password you wish to automatically log on with, and then click **OK**.
5. Click **OK** again and you're all done.

Enable Hibernation Mode For Your Computer

Hibernation mode saves the current state of your computer to its hard drive before powering off. The next time you press the power button, the computer starts in the same state in which you left it.

Using hibernation mode can save you some time starting your system. It doesn't need to boot from scratch, instead it just "wakes-up" from a deep sleep. The advantage is that it resumes where it left off.

To enable hibernation support on your computer:

1. You must be logged on as an administrator or a member of the Administrators or Power Users group.
2. Click **Start**, click **Control Panel**, click **Performance and Maintenance**, and then click **Power Options**.
3. Click the **Hibernate** tab, and then select the **Enable hibernate support** check box. If the **Hibernate** tab is not available, your hardware does not support this feature.
4. Click **OK** to close the **Power Options** dialog box.

Manually Put Your System Into Hibernation

If you are using Windows XP Home Edition, or Windows XP Professional with Fast User Switching turned on, the Turn Off Computer menu only displays the **Stand By**, **Turn Off**, or **Restart** your computer options. You can reveal the **Hibernate** button with a simple keystroke.

To manually place your computer into hibernation, after enabling hibernation on your computer, follow this tip:

1. Click **Start**, and then click **Shutdown**.
2. Press and hold the **SHIFT** key. The label under the first button on the left changes from **Stand By to Hibernate**.
3. Click the **Hibernate** button.

Burning Your Own CD-ROMs

If you're running Windows XP, then you don't have to go out and buy expensive CD-recording software. It already has support for CD burning. You only need to a have a CD-ROM recorder.

When you want to burn a CD using Windows XP:

1. Insert a blank CD–R or CD–RW in your CD drive. A dialog box opens, asking if you want to open a writable CD folder. Click **OK**.
2. On the **Start** menu, click **My Computer**, and navigate to the drive and folder where the files you wish to copy are stored.
3. Select the files you wish to copy, and drag/drop or copy/paste them to the open CD recording folder.
4. In the left pane of the CD folder window, click **Write these files to CD**.

Just remember not to copy more files than a CD will hold, which is typically 650 MB.

How To Hide/Unhide A File Or Folder

You can protect a file or folder by hiding it, or unhide a system file so you can edit it. Here's how to hide a file:

1. Double-click **My Computer**.
2. Navigate to the file you want to hide/unhide.
3. Right click on the file then click **Properties**.
4. Click the **General** tab and select the **Hidden** check box.
5. Click **Apply**, then **OK**.
6. To view hidden files, click the **Tools** menu in any folder window, then click **Folder Options**.
7. Click the **View** tab, under **Advanced settings**, select **Show hidden files and folders** as shown in Figure 10.

How To Hide/Unhide A File Or Folder, Cont.

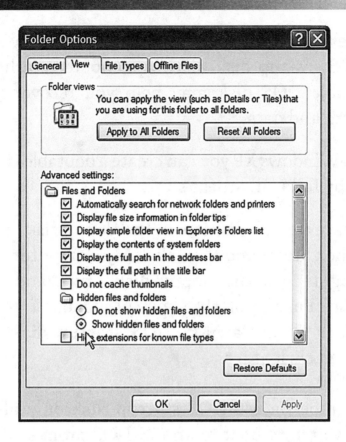

Figure 10: Hide properties dialog box

Create An MS-DOS Startup Disk

Yes, even in today's Windows world you may need a DOS startup disk. If your computer crashes, a bootable DOS disk may help you recover your system and data.

With Windows XP you can create a bootable floppy disk by following these steps:

1. Place a blank diskette in the floppy disk drive.
2. Click **Start**, and then click **My Computer**.
3. Right–click the floppy disk drive, and then click **Format** on the shortcut menu.
4. Click **Create an MS–DOS startup disk**, and then click **Start**.

Remember, a MS-DOS startup disk only allows the system to boot to an MS-DOS prompt. It is a good tool for troubleshooting your computer.

Speed Up Windows Menu Display

Here is a tip to speed up menu display in Windows XP.

1. Click **Start**, click **Control Panel**, the select **System**.
2. Click the **Advanced** tab.
3. Under **Performance**, click the **Settings** button.
4. Clear the **Fade or slide** menus into view check box, and then click **OK**.

This tip configures a collapsed menu to expand without delay.

Find A Lost File Or Folder

It happens to all of us. We misplace a file or folder and cannot find it anywhere on our computer. Windows XP has an excellent search tool to help you locate it.

To search for a file or folder:

1. Click **Start**, and then click **Search**.
2. Click **All files and folders**.
3. Type part or all of the name of the file or folder, or type a word or phrase that is in the file. You can narrow your search with the following options:
   - In **Look in**, click the drive, folder, or network you want to search.
   - Click **When was it modified?** Look for files that were created or modified on or between specific dates.
   - Click **What size is it?** to look for files of a specific size.
   - Click **More advanced options** to specify additional search criteria.
4. Click **Search**.

Require A Password To Log On

You can require users of your computer to login before they can gain access to it.

This configuration is helpful if you share a computer with friends or family. It also allows them to set up their own Windows environment without affecting others.

Here's how to configure XP to require logins:

1. Click **Start** and choose **Control Panel**.
2. Double click the **User Accounts** icon.
3. Check the **Users must enter a username and password to use this computer** check box.
4. Click **Apply**.

Use Keyboard Shortcuts To Open A Folder

If you have a folder that you access frequently, try creating a keyboard shortcut to open it with a few keystrokes. Here's how:

1. Select the folder in Windows Explorer.
2. Create a shortcut, and place it on the desktop. You create a shortcut by opening the folder, pointing to **New** on the **File** menu, then clicking **Shortcut**. Drag the shortcut to your desktop.
3. Right–click the new shortcut, and then click **Properties**. You could also press the **Menu** key on your keyboard.
4. In the **Properties** dialog box, click the **Shortcut** tab, and in the **Shortcut** key box, enter a **CTRL** key combination or a **CTRL+SHIFT** key combination, (that is, **CTRL+ALT+T** or **CTRL+SHIFT+T**), and then click **OK**.

Use Your Own Pictures As Your Wallpaper

Make your favorite photo or image the background wallpaper on your desktop with these steps:

1. Find the desired picture or image using Windows Explorer.
2. Right-click on the image file, and then click **Preview** to open it in Image Viewer.
3. Right-click again on the image, and select **Set as Wallpaper**.
4. Depending on your image viewer, you may have to click on **Tools**, to find the **Set as Wallpaper** command.

Monitor System Performance

Windows XP has a handy utility for monitoring system performance. To access this utility:

1. Press **CTRL+ALT+DEL** on your keyboard.
2. Choose **Task Manager**.
3. Select the **Performance** tab once it loads. You will see two real-time graphs of your system's performance. The window should resemble Figure 11. The top graph is CPU usage and the bottom is the total amount of used memory.

If any of these lines hover around the top of the graph for an extended period of time, you should consider restarting your computer. You will probably notice your computer is very slow during this time.

Restarting your system will stop whatever program is taxing your system.

Monitor System Performance, Cont.

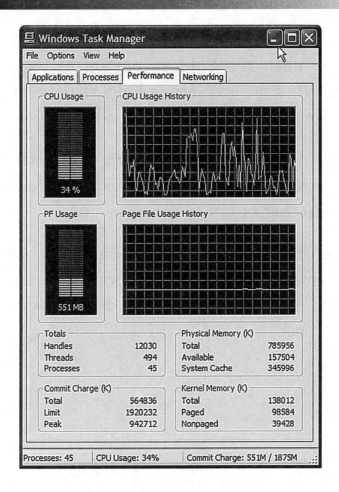

Figure 11: Task manager showing
system performance

Toggle The Folders Tree

Regardless of the view you use for a given folder, you can click the **Folders** button to toggle between Windows Explorer's Folders pane and the Task Pane.

Use the double arrows at the right of each menu in the Task Pane to collapse or expand the choices shown in that box.

In the Details box, the double arrow toggles the display of information about the currently selected file or folder (including previews of image files).

Different Ways To Delete Files And Folders

Windows XP gives you several ways to remove the files and folders you don't want.

Using Windows Explorer, you can use any of these methods to delete a file or files:

- Right–click the file or folder, then click the **DELETE** key.
- Select the file or folder, then press the **DELETE** key.
- Select the file or folder, click the **File** menu, and then click **DELETE**.
- Drag the file or folder to the **Recycle Bin** on the desktop.

Remember, to completely remove the file you must empty your Recycle Bin by right clicking it and choosing **Empty Recycle Bin**.

Display The Volume Control Icon
In The Taskbar

You can place a shortcut on your taskbar to the volume control. This allows you to easily adjust the volume without having to open the control panel. Follow these steps to create the shortcut:

1. Click **Start**, and then click **Control Panel**.
2. Click **Sound, Speech, and Audio Devices**.
3. On the **Volume** tab, in the **Device and Volume** area select the **Place volume icon in the taskbar** check box, and then click **Apply** and **OK**.

Now, when you want to adjust the volume, click the volume control icon in the system tray and move the slider.

It's loudest at the top and softest at the bottom. You can also make it completely quiet by clicking the **Mute** check box.

Display Your Quick Launch Toolbar

The Quick Launch bar displays shortcuts you can click to quickly open programs, show the desktop, or perform other tasks. It is located on the taskbar at the bottom of your screen.

To display the Quick Launch toolbar just right-click an empty area on the taskbar, click **Toolbars**, and then click **Quick Launch**. To add items to your Quick Launch toolbar, click the icon for the program you want to add, and drag it to the Quick Launch portion of the taskbar.

Customize Your Mouse And Pointer

Tired of your mouse pointer being an arrow or hourglass? Then try a different pointer scheme, such as Dinosaur, Ocean or Sports.

Change your mouse pointer this way:

1. Open the Control Panel, double-click **Mouse**. If you start the Control Panel in Category view, select **Appearance and Themes**, then click **Mouse Pointers** under **See Also**.
2. Select the **Pointers** tab.
3. Next to **Schemes**, click the down arrow and select a scheme to preview its pointers. See Figure 12.
4. Click **OK** to apply the scheme to your desktop.

Customize Your Mouse And Pointer, Cont.

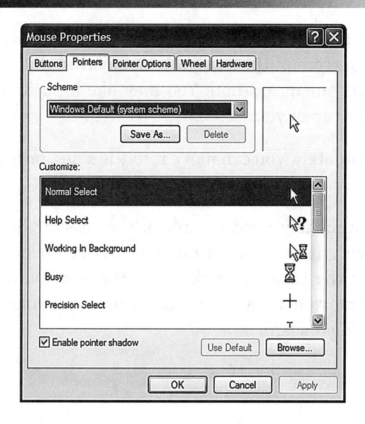

Figure 12: Mouse pointer configuration

Relocate Your Taskbar

By default, Windows XP places the taskbar at the bottom of the screen. You may find this is an inconvenient location. You may like it positioned at the top of your screen.

Fortunately, you can move it to the sides, or top of your screen! Whatever works best for you.

You probably need to unlock the taskbar before moving it. Right-click on the taskbar, then click **Lock the taskbar** to clear the check mark. Once you move it where you want, you might consider locking it again.

Auto-Hide Your Taskbar

To get the most viewing area on your monitor, you can choose to auto-hide the taskbar. The taskbar will disappear when your mouse pointer isn't over it.

To use this function:

1. Right click the taskbar.
2. Choose **Properties**.
3. Check **Auto-hide the taskbar** checkbox.
4. Click **OK**.

Use Mouse Trails To Make It Easy To View The Mouse

Enabling mouse trails makes it easier to see your mouse when it is moving. This causes the mouse to leave a short trail of "footprints" to help you track it as it moves.

Here is how to enable mouse trails:

1. Click the **Start Menu**, then click the **Control Panel**.
2. Double-click **Mouse** to open the **Mouse Properties** dialog box.
3. Select the **Pointer Options** tab.
4. Under **Visibility** click the **Display pointer trails** check box. See Figure 13.
5. You can adjust the length of the trail moving the arrow on the slider.
6. Select **OK**.

Use Mouse Trails To Make It Easy To View The Mouse, Cont.

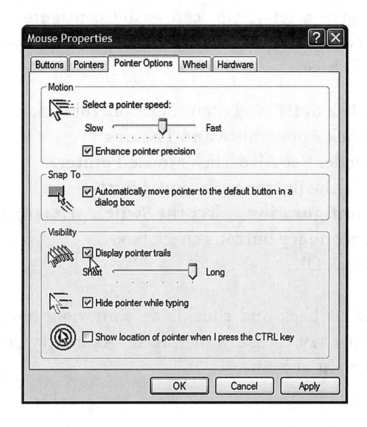

Figure 13: Mouse trails dialog box

Make A Left-Handed Mouse

If you're a lefty, you can easily configure your mouse so you can use it with your left hand. Here's how:

1. Click **Start**, and then click **Control Panel**.
2. Click **Appearance and Themes**.
3. Under **See Also**, click **Mouse Pointers**.
4. On the **Buttons** tab, under **Button configuration**, select the **Switch primary and secondary buttons** check box.
5. Click **OK**.

Now sit back and chuckle as your right-handed friends try to use your mouse. As a lefty you'll feel right at home.

Change The Speed Of Your Mouse

For some people, the speed at which the mouse moves across the screen is too fast. If it is too fast or too slow, simply change it. Here's how:

1. Click **Start**, and then click **Control Panel**.
2. Click **Appearance and Themes**.
3. Under **See Also**, click **Mouse Pointers**.
4. On the **Pointer Options** tab, under Motion, drag the slider left to make the pointer move slower, or right to make the pointer move faster. You can test the speed as you make the adjustment.
5. Click **OK** when satisfied.

Top Ten Windows XP Keyboard Shortcuts

The following is a list of ten very useful Windows XP keyboard shortcuts. Memorize and use these to increase your productivity.

- **CTRL+C** – copies selected item.

- **CTRL+X** – cuts selected item.

- **CTRL+V** – paste data from clipboard to active application.

- **ALT+TAB** – cycle between open Windows.

- **CTRL+ALT+DEL** – opens a dialog box with system management options such as Shutdown and Restart.

- **CTRL+F4** – closes active window.

- **CTRL+A** – selects everything in a window.

- **CTRL+P** – opens the Print dialog box.

- **F1** – displays Help system.

- **F2** – rename a selected item such as a file or folder.

How To Increase Icon Size

Sometimes icons are tough to see, especially if you use a high screen resolution. XP lets you make the icons larger so they will be easier to see.

To make your icons larger:

1. Click **Start**, and then click **Control Panel**.
2. Click **Appearance and Themes**.
3. Select **Display**, to open the **Display Properties** dialog box.
4. Click the **Appearance** tab then click the **Effects** button.
5. Select **Use large icons** check box as shown in Figure 14.
6. Click **OK**, then **OK** again.

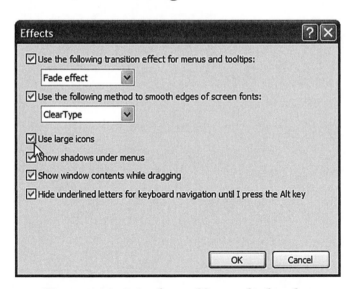

Figure 14: Display effects dialog box

Enable Automatic Windows Updates

It is very important to keep Windows XP updated with security patches from Microsoft. It is so important that XP automatically does it for you.

To configure automatic updates (or change the current settings):

1. Click **Start**.
2. Click **Control Panel**.
3. Double-click **System**.
4. On the **Automatic Updates** tab, click either of the first two settings.

PART 2

Internet Explorer Shortcuts and Tips

Microsoft Internet Explorer (IE) is Windows XP's default browser. It has a lot of features and tools that make browsing the Web easier and quicker.

You can customize IE to suit your needs. In this Part we cover how to configure IE to meet your needs and provide tips to speed-up your surfing. Topics range from changing font sizes to disabling pop-up advertisements.

Everyone should find an interesting tip in this Part.

Copy Text From A Web Page

You can cut and paste text from a Web site just like you can from other applications.

To copy text from a Web page, drag the mouse across text to select it and then press **CTRL+C** to copy it.

This method is fine unless you need to select a large body of text. In this case, you can click at the left side of the beginning word in the text and then hold **SHIFT** key down while you click after the last word of the text. Press **CTRL+C**.

Pressing **CTRL+V** pastes it into your application.

Find Relevant Information In A
Long Web Page

You might stumble across a Web site you think has the information you need, but the page is really long; or it may be too long to read in the amount of time you have.

Fortunately, you can search a Web page just like you search a Word document. Try this:

1. Press **CTRL+F** and Microsoft Internet Explorer opens the **Find** dialog box.
2. Type in your phrase (and search conditions).
3. Click **Find Next**.

This should take you to the information you were looking for.

Accessing FTP Sites Using Internet Explorer

If a Web site lets you download files, such as software updates or audio files, it may be using either FTP or http. This is a good thing because FTP downloads are much faster than http.

Usually you need FTP client software to download these files. However, did you know that you can use Microsoft Internet Explorer to access FTP sites on the Internet?

If you enter an FTP address into the Microsoft Internet Explorer Address Bar, the browser will navigate to that site. To enter an FTP address just type ftp:// instead of http://, Internet Explorer will do the rest.

If an FTP site requires a username and password, Internet Explorer will prompt you for this information. For example, you might be asked for a username and password if you are downloading account information from a financial institution.

Control Long Page Loads In Internet Explorer

When a Web page takes a long time to download its graphics, press the **Spacebar** to stop the graphics and just load the text. You can always refresh the page if you must see the graphics.

You could also try clicking the **Stop** button and then clicking the **Refresh** (or press **F5**). Starting the download again might improve your download speed.

Note that you can't stop file downloads by clicking **Stop**. To stop a file download, click **Cancel** in the **Download** dialog box.

Customize Internet Explorer Toolbar Buttons

Internet Explorer has lots of toolbar buttons for doing various tasks. However, you can add or subtract buttons to make the toolbar more useful to you. Here's how:

1. Click the **View** menu, click **Toolbars,** and click **Customize.** In the **Customize Toolbar** box, you have lots of options for adding, removing, and rearranging buttons. Figure 15 shows the **Customize Toolbar** dialog box.
2. Click a button in **Available toolbar buttons** list and click the **Add** button to place the button on the toolbar.
3. Click a button from the list of **Current toolbar buttons**, and click the **Remove** button to delete the button from the toolbar.
4. You can rearrange the buttons by clicking on a button from the **Current toolbar buttons** list, then clicking **Move Up** and **Move Down**.
5. When finished, click the **Close** button.

Customize Internet Explorer
Toolbar Buttons, Cont.

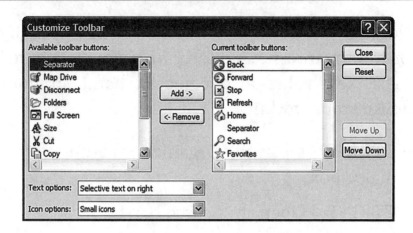

Figure 15: Customize the IE toolbar dialog box

Navigating The Web With The Keyboard

Did you know that you can surf the Web by controlling Internet Explorer with your keyboard? These keystrokes also come in handy if your mouse stops working.

- **CTRL+B** – Open the Organize Favorites dialog box.

- **CTRL+E** – Open the Search bar.

- **CTRL+F** – Start the Find utility.

- **CTRL+H** – Open the History sidebar.

- **CTRL+I** – Open the Favorites sidebar.

- **CTRL+L** – Open the Open dialog box.

- **CTRL+N** – Start another instance of the browser with the same Web address.

- **CTRL+O** – Open the Open dialog box, the same as CTRL+L.

- **CTRL+P** – Open the Print dialog box.

- **CTRL+R** – Update the current Web page.

- **CTRL+W** – Close the current window.

- **BACKSPACE** – Go back to the previous page.

- **ALT+F4** – Close Internet Explorer.

Install The Google Toolbar

Google provides a feature-rich toolbar for Internet Explorer. It allows you to do searches without first navigating to Google and also has a powerful pop-up ad blocker as well as shortcuts to some of Google's popular tools.

Here is how to download and install the Google Toolbar:

1. Start Microsoft Internet Explorer.
2. Enter **http://toolbar.google.com/** in the Address Bar.
3. Click the "**Download Google Toolbar**" button.
4. After the download screen appears, choose **Open**.
5. Read the "**Toolbar Terms of Use**", and click **Agree**.
6. Follow the instructions to install the toolbar. When finished, the toolbar appears at the top of your Internet Explorer screen.

Install The Yahoo! Toolbar

Like Google, Yahoo! provides a toolbar for Internet Explorer. To install the toolbar:

1. Start Microsoft Internet Explorer.
2. Enter **http://toolbar.yahoo.com/** in the Address Bar.
3. Click the **Download Yahoo! Toolbar** button.
4. Click **Yes** to start the Yahoo! install manager.
5. Follow the instructions to install the toolbar. When finished, the Yahoo! Toolbar appears at the top of your Internet Explorer screen.

Forget Typing http

You no longer need to prefix an Internet site's address with http:// when typing it in the Address Bar.

This technique will save you some typing. Especially since http:// is not that easy to type.

Add A Web Site To Your Favorites
With One Keystroke

Quickly adding a Web page to your Favorites folder is simple.

Just press **CTRL+D** and the page is automatically added to your Favorites list.

Alphabetize Your Favorites List

By default, your favorite Web sites are listed in the order that you saved them. This behavior can make it difficult to find anything in this list.

Here's how to alphabetize them for easier access:

1. Click the **Favorites Menu**.
2. Right-click on any of your Favorites items.
3. Click **Sort by Name**.

Your Favorites List should now be listed in alphabetical order.

You can also create folders in your Favorites list and place related items in the folder. This helps to keep the Favorites list uncluttered.

Open Link In A New Window

How often have you wanted to follow a link, but didn't want to lose the Web page you were reading? The solution is to open the link in a new browser window. Here are two ways to do it:

Method 1 — Hold the **SHIFT** key down while clicking on the link.

Method 2 — Right-click on the link and choose **Open in New Window**.

How To Increase Font Size In Internet Explorer

How often have you visited a Web site that is hard to read? Either everything is crammed together or the font is too small.

Did you know that IE will let you change the font size on the Web page? Here are two ways to do it:

1. Click **View** on the menu bar.
2. Click **Text Size**.
3. Choose **Large** or **Largest**.

Try this approach if you have a wheel mouse:

1. Hold the **CTRL** button.
2. Rotate the mouse wheel to increase or decrease the size as appropriate.

How To Clear Temporary Internet Files

Internet Explorer uses temporary files to speed-up your Web access by storing recently viewed pages and images on your hard drive.

As you might imagine, this can take up quite a bit of disk space over time. Here is how to reclaim the space occupied by temporary files:

1. Click **Tools** on the **Menu** bar.
2. Click **Internet Options**.
3. Click the **General** tab.
4. Under **Temporary Internet Files** click the **Delete Files** button as shown in Figure 16.
5. Click the **Delete all offline content** check box.
6. Click the **OK** button.
7. Click the **OK** button again.

How To Clear Temporary Internet Files, Cont.

Figure 16: Clear Internet Explorer temporary files

Automatically Clear Temporary Internet Files

If you wish, Internet Explorer can clear its temporary Internet files when it closes. Here's how to enable that behavior:

1. Go to **Tools** then choose **Internet Options**.
2. Click on the **Advanced** button.
3. Scroll down almost to the bottom and check, **Empty Temporary Internet Files** folder when browser is closed.
4. Click **OK**.

How To Clear Your Surfing History

Internet Explorer tracks the Web sites you have visited. Clicking the **History** button on the toolbar displays a list of most recently visited Web sites.

If you want to delete your surfing history:

1. Click **Tools** on the **Menu** bar.
2. Click **Internet Options**.
3. Click the **General** tab.
4. Under **History** click the **Clear History** button.
5. Click the **Yes** button on the next dialog box.
6. Click the **OK** button.

How To Use Pop-Up Ad Blocking

There is little argument about the annoyance of pop-up ads when surfing the Internet. To reduce their impact, Internet Explorer has a pop-up ad blocker.

This feature is turned off by default but easily enabled. Here's how:

1. Click **Tools** on the **Menu** bar and choose **Pop-up Blocker**.
2. Click **Turn On Pop-up Blocker**.
3. Click **Tools** again and choose **Pop-up Blocker**.
4. Click **Pop-up Blocker Settings** to reveal the dialog box show in Figure 17.
5. Choose a **Filter level** setting at the bottom of the dialog box. We use the **High** setting to block all pop-ups. If you encounter a site with a pop-up you want to see, press the **CTRL** button while clicking a link or refreshing the page. This overrides the setting.
6. Click **OK**.

The inconvenience of the highest filter setting is well worth it. Hackers can use pop-up windows to load spyware and other malicious programs. It's better to be a little inconvenienced than hacked.

How To Use Pop-Up Ad Blocking, Cont.

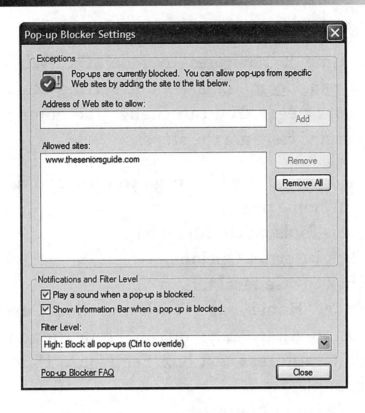

Figure 17: Pop-up blocker settings

How To Change Your Home Page

When you open Internet Explorer for the first time it navigates to MSNBC's Web site, www.msnbc.com. This default setting may not suit your needs. You can change the home page very easily. Here are the steps:

1. Navigate to the Web page you want to use as your home page.
2. Click **Tools** on the **Menu** bar.
3. Click **Internet Options**.
4. Click the **General** tab.
5. Under **Home page**, click the **Use Current** button. Alternately, you could type the address in the **Address** text box. See Figure 18 for an example.
6. Click the **OK** button.

How To Change Your Home Page, Cont.

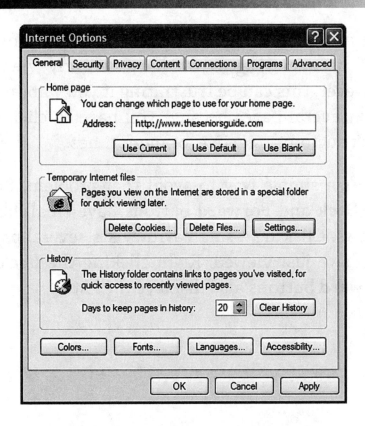

Figure 18: Setting a custom home page

Navigating Back And Forward

You can click the **Back** and **Forward** buttons to surf between pages you have recently viewed. However, this can be frustrating if you want to go back several pages because you have to click the **Back** button three, five, or more times.

Here's a simple way to avoid that problem. Both the **Back** and **Forward** buttons have small black arrows. Clicking a small arrow lists several pages you have just viewed. Right-clicking the **Back** or **Forward** buttons also displays the list.

Two Ways To Refresh A Web Page

To speed up page loads from a Web site, Internet Explorer may save images and some text on your hard drive. The next time you navigate the site, it will reuse those elements already downloaded. This behavior is called "caching."

For obvious reasons, you will likely want the most current content. If you are reading a financial site, you will want to refresh the Web page to keep the most current data.

Here are two ways to refresh a Web page:

- Press **F5**.

- Click **View** on the menu bar then click **Refresh**.

Use Internet Explorer In Full-Screen Mode

To further enhance your browsing experience, try viewing a Web page at full screen. In doing so, Internet Explorer will occupy your entire monitor screen.

To make Internet Explorer use the entire monitor, press **F11**. Internet Explorer will expand to fill your screen. To reset Internet Explorer back to normal, just press **F11** again.

This trick works great when viewing images, reading online newspapers, or watching videos.

Use CTRL+ENTER To Complete
Web Site Addresses

Save yourself some typing by letting Internet Explorer enter the **www** and **.com** into the Address Bar by typing the name of the page and pressing **CTRL+ENTER** on the keyboard.

For example if you type **theseniorsguide** and press **CTRL+ENTER** you will automatically be sent to our Web site; www.theseniorsguide.com.

Turn Off The Internet Explorer Clicking Sound

Does the clicking sound Internet Explorer makes when you click on a link irritate you? Don't worry, to turn off that annoying click:

1. Click the **Start Menu**.
2. Click **Control Panel**.
3. Choose **Sounds and Audio devices**.
4. Click the **Sounds** tab.
5. Scroll down to Windows Explorer and in the sub menu, highlight **Start navigation**.
6. In the drop down box below, where it currently says **Start** or **Windows Start** and choose '**(none)**' instead.
7. Click **Apply**.
8. Click **OK**, and close the **Control Panel**.

You should not hear any more clicking.

Browsing Tips With A Scroll Mouse

A wheel mouse, sometimes called a scroll mouse, can greatly aid your surfing. Here are two tips on how to use it when browsing with Internet Explorer:

- Hold **CTRL** and rotate the scroll wheel on the mouse to increase or decrease the font size.
- Hold **SHIFT** and rotate the scroll wheel to go back or forward between Web pages.

Saving Pictures In Internet Explorer

If you see an image on a Web site that you like, you can save it to your hard drive.

1. Right-click on the picture.
2. Choose **Save Picture As**. You usually have two file format choices, the original picture format or BMP. If the picture at the Web site was originally saved in GIF, then your choices are GIF and BMP.
3. Pick your destination folder and click the **Save** button.

PART 3

Microsoft Word

This Part has tips and tricks for Microsoft Word for Windows, or more commonly referred to as Word.

Most tips work with either Word 2000, Word XP, or Word 2003. Some will work with older versions of Word, such as Word 97.

How To Get Word To Stop
Helping Me Type

Word tries to help you in many different ways. One way is to autocorrect words as you type. This feature is enabled by default. If this annoys you, here is how to turn it off:

1. Choose **AutoCorrect** (or **AutoCorrect Options**) from the **Tools** menu, then click on the **AutoCorrect** tab.
2. Clear the check boxes for the **AutoCorrect** items that you want to disable. See Figure 19.
3. Choose **OK**.

How To Get Word To Stop
Helping Me Type, Cont.

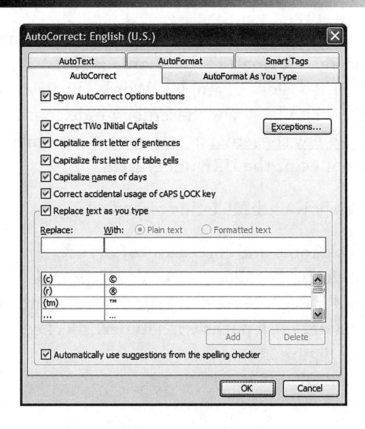

Figure 19: AutoCorrect dialog box

How To Turn Off The Automatic URL Formatting

When you type a URL in Word it is automatically formatted as an HTML hypertext link. For example, Word displays our Web site www.theseniorsguide.com as http://www.theseniorsguide.com. You may or may not want the URL underlined.

Here is how to disable this feature:

1. Click **Tools** and choose **AutoCorrect**.
2. Click the **AutoFormat As You Type** tab.
3. Under **Replace As You Type**, clear the **Internet and network paths with hyperlink** check box. See Figure 20.
4. Click **OK**.

How To Turn Off The Automatic URL Formatting, Cont.

Figure 20: AutoFormat dialog box

How To Turn Off The Office Assistant

Office Assistant is meant to be an interactive help system and is enabled by default. More often than not it gets in the way by taking up screen space and using processor power. Follow these steps to turn off Office Assistant:

1. Click on the **Office Assistant**, then click on **Options**.
2. Clear the **Use Office Assistant** check box.
3. Click **OK**.

Find Out The Name Of Toolbar Buttons

Word's toolbars have a lot of buttons and text boxes. You may wonder what these buttons are called. We certainly do and we use Word everyday!

To find out what the buttons are; hover the mouse pointer over any button and its name will appear in a box near the mouse pointer. See Figure 21 below for an example:

Figure 21: Toolbar button name

Find Out What Toolbar Buttons Do

You may wonder what some of the toolbar buttons do. Here is an easy way to get an overview of a button's purpose:

1. Click the **Help** menu and choose **What's This?**, which turns the mouse pointer into a "**?**."
2. Click on any button, or any other object and Word will give you some information.

A keyboard shortcut you can use, **SHIFT+F1**, will turn on the "**What's This?**" feature.

Turn The Ruler On And Off

If you have a large document, you may want to view as much of it as you can. To gain some space in Word's workspace you can turn the ruler off.

It's simple to do, just click the **View** menu and choose **Ruler**. The checkmark will disappear. Clicking **Ruler** again will make Word display it.

How To Display More Toolbars

Microsoft Word has many toolbars and you can choose to view all or none of them. Here's how to control which toolbars are displayed:

1. Click the **View** menu and choose **Toolbars**.
2. Click the toolbar you want to view. Active toolbars have a check next to their names.

You can hide a toolbar by clicking an active tool-bar (the one with a checkmark) in the menu. This will remove the checkmark next to its name and the toolbar will disappear.

How To Move The Word Toolbars

Since Word has lots of toolbars, if you use more than a couple you might start cluttering up Word's work area. To combat this problem, Word allows you to move a toolbar to a more convenient location.

Here's how:

1. Click on the left edge of the toolbar (the mouse pointer will turn into a four-headed pointer).
2. Drag the toolbar to any edge for a toolbar or anywhere else on the screen for a floating palette.

How To Add Toolbar Buttons

Do you have a Menu command, such as Copy or Paste that you use often? If so, consider adding it to a toolbar for easier access. Follow these steps to add it to a toolbar:

1. Click **View** then choose **Toolbars**.
2. Click **Customize**.
3. Click on the **Commands** tab.
4. Select an item under **Categories**.
5. Select an item from the list of **Commands**.
6. Drag the command to a toolbar. An "**I**" beam will appear to help you install the button. By default, the new button has only a text label. See Figure 22 on the next page.
7. Right-click on the new **Toolbar** item.
8. Select **Default Style** (the button will become a plain square).
9. Right click on the new **Toolbar** item again.
10. Choose **Change Button Image**, then select a button image.
11. Close the **Customize** dialog box.

How To Add Toolbar Buttons, Cont.

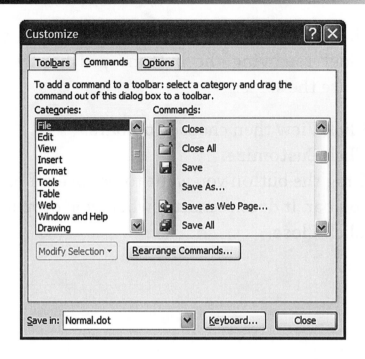

Figure 22: Customize Word toolbar dialog

How To Remove Toolbar Buttons

If all the buttons on the toolbars confuse you, consider removing the buttons you hardly use. Here are the steps:

1. Click **View** then choose **Toolbars**.
2. Click **Customize**.
3. Drag the button you want to remove off of the toolbar. It doesn't matter where you drop it.
4. Click **Close**.

How To Make Custom Toolbars

If you desire, you can make a custom toolbar with only the buttons you use most frequently.

Here are the steps:

1. Click **View** then choose **Toolbars**.
2. Click **Customize**.
3. Click on the **Toolbars** tab, then click on the **New** button.
4. Give your new toolbar a name.
5. Make the toolbar available to the **Normal** template (all documents).
6. Click **OK**. A small toolbar palette will appear on the screen.
7. Click on the **Commands** tab, select a **Category**, then drag the commands you want onto your new toolbar.
8. Click **Close**.

Your new toolbar should be ready for use!

How To Customize Menus

Just like you can customize Word's toolbars, you can customize its menus as well. Here's how to do it:

1. Click **View** then choose **Toolbars**.
2. Click **Customize**.
3. Once the **Customize** dialog box is open you can drag unwanted items off any of the menus.
4. To add a command to a menu click on the **Commands** tab.
5. Select a **Category**, then drag the command you want onto any of the menus.

To restore a menu to its original setup, follow the steps above, but right-click on the menu you want to restore and select **Reset**.

What Is The Normal Template?

Word uses the "Normal" template when creating a new document. The Normal template controls the default margins, font size, font style, bullet type, and most of all other formatting aspects of a Word document.

When you modify the Normal template, all new documents you create will include those modifications. Word keeps the Normal template file (Normal.dot) in the Template folder (contained in the folder where you have installed Microsoft Office).

If you accidentally delete the Normal template file, Word creates a new one with the default settings the next time it starts.

How To Change The Margins

Most of the time Word's default margins are adequate. Sometimes though you may want to increase or decrease them to improve the look of your document or squeeze more lines onto your page.

Here's how to manipulate Word's margins:

1. Click **File**.
2. Click **Page Setup**.
3. Click the **Margins** tab.
4. Enter the settings you want for the **Top**, **Bottom**, **Left**, and **Right** margin. You can ignore the **Gutter** setting unless you are formatting a document as a book or multi-page newsletter.
5. Choose **Whole document** in the **Apply to** combo-box.
6. Click **OK**.

If you don't like your settings, repeat the process except click the **Default...** button to reset the margins. Alternately, you can press **CTRL+Z** to undo the margin setting.

How To Set Tabs In A Word Document

Word sets the tab stops at one-half inch as a default. Like most formatting options in Word, you can change that setting too. Here is how:

1. Make sure you can see the ruler at the top of the document. If you don't, click **View** and choose **Ruler**. It should have a checkmark next to it.
2. To set a tab click on the ruler at the spot where you want the tab. A little "**L**" should appear on the ruler.
3. To remove a tab mark, click on the "**L**" and pull it off the ruler.

You can change the type of tab justification (left, right, or center) by clicking on the little box with a tab mark in it. Clicking it rotates through the different tab justifications.

Note: Word's default tab stops, at ½ inch intervals, do not appear on the ruler.

How To Change The Font In A Word Document

Changing the font in Word is easy. There are two methods to choose from.

Method 1:

1. Ensure the Formatting Toolbar is viewable. Click **View**, choose **Toolbars** and see if there is a checkmark next to the **Formatting** toolbar.
2. The **Formatting** toolbar has three combo-boxes, the middle box controls the font.
3. Click the **down-arrow** on the font combo-box and choose a new font from the list.

Now everything you type will appear as that font.

Method 2:

1. Choose **Format**, click **Font**.
2. Pick a new font from the list.
3. Click **OK**.

If you want to change the font of an existing word or text block, highlight the word(s) and change the font as described above.

How To Change The Font For Existing Text

Did you know that you can change the formatting of text you have already written? You may want to experiment with fonts and styles to make your document look the best it can.

To change formatting of existing text, just select the region you want to change and follow the procedures for changing fonts, colors, etc. You can use your mouse or keyboard to make the selections.

How To Make Bold Or Italic Text

Making bold text in Word is simple. Choose from two methods:

Method 1:

1. Ensure the **Formatting** toolbar is viewable. Click **View**, choose **Toolbars** and see if there is a checkmark next to the **Formatting** toolbar.
2. Click the **B** for bold, or *I* for italics, and now everything you type will appear bold or italics respectively.

Method 2:

1. Choose **Format**, click **Font**.
2. Click **Bold** or *Italic* under **Font style**.
3. Click **OK**.

If you want to make an existing word or text block bold, highlight the word(s) and change the font as described above.

How To Underline Text

Underlining text in Word is as easy as making it bold or italicized. Just like the other formatting techniques, you can choose from two methods:

Method 1:

1. Ensure the **Formatting** Toolbar is viewable. Click **View**, choose **Toolbars** and see if there is a checkmark next to the **Formatting** toolbar.
2. Click the "**U**" and now everything you type will be underlined.

Method 2:

1. Choose **Format**, click **Font**.
2. Choose an underline style from the **Underline style** dropdown list.
3. Click **OK**.

If you want to underline an existing word or text block, highlight the word(s) and change it as described above.

How To Change The Font Color

Word lets you format your text in any color you wish. Like the other techniques, you can choose from two methods:

Method 1:

1. Ensure the **Formatting** toolbar is viewable. Click **View**, choose **Toolbars** and see if there is a checkmark next to the **Formatting** toolbar.
2. Click the down arrow next to the "**A**". A color palette appears from which you can choose a color. Now everything you type will appear as that color. The "**A**" appears as the current color.
3. To reset the color, choose the **Automatic** setting.

Method 2:

1. Choose **Format**, click **Font**.
2. Choose a color from the **Font** color dropdown box.
3. Click **OK**.

If you want to change the color of an existing word or text block, highlight the word(s) and change the color as described above.

How To Change The Default Folder

You may decide to keep your Word documents in a different folder than My Documents. This is probably wise as it helps keep your files organized. However, it is annoying when you have to navigate to the document folder every time you need to open a file.

Here is how to solve that problem:

1. Choose **Options** from the **Tools** menu.
2. Click on the **File Locations** tab.
3. Click on **Documents** under **File Types**.
4. Click on the **Modify** button.
5. Use the **Look in** list to locate the folder you want to use from now on.
6. Click on the folder name, then click on **OK** to select that location.
7. Click on **OK**.

How To Use AutoText

AutoText is like shorthand and provides a way to quickly insert text, graphics, fields, tables, bookmarks, and other items that you use frequently. Word comes with a library of AutoText entries. You can create your own AutoText entries with the following method:

1. Choose **AutoCorrect** or **AutoCorrect Options** (depending upon your Word version) from the **Tools** menu, then click on the **AutoText** tab.
2. Type the text of your new **AutoText** entry in the **Enter AutoText** entries here box, then click on **Add**. See Figure 23.
3. Make sure the **Show AutoComplete** tip check box is checked.
4. Click **OK**.

How To Use AutoText, Cont.

Figure 23: AutoText dialog box

How To Find Word's Keyboard Shortcuts

Word has a lot of keyboard shortcuts. Word uses a built-in macro to create a document that lists the shortcuts.

Follow these steps to get a list of shortcuts:

1. Choose **Macro** from the **Tools** menu, then choose **Macros**.
2. Select **Word** commands from the list in the **Macros** in box.
3. From the list in the **Macro** name box, choose **List Commands** (you can type a lower-case "L" to jump to that section).
4. Click **Run**.

In the **List Commands** dialog box, click **Current menu and keyboard settings**.

The macro will run, generating a document in table form that you can print. Be forewarned, it is pretty long. There are ten pages of shortcuts, organized alphabetically by command name.

How To Clear All Text Formatting

If you are trying to format a block of text and it is not looking like you want, then reset it to the way it was by:

1. Selecting the block of text.
2. Choosing **Normal** from the **Style** box. Anything that doesn't go away will have to be reformatted with the appropriate character or paragraph formatting commands.

How To View Formatting Marks

If your document doesn't look like you think it should you can look at the hidden format marks to troubleshoot the problem.

You can use the **Show/Hide** button [¶] on the Standard toolbar to display paragraph marks, tabs, and spaces. Paragraph marks appear as ¶, spaces as "·", and tabs as "→".

How To Double-Space A Document

By default, Word single spaces your document. If you need it double-spaced:

1. Select the portion of the document that you want double-spaced. To select the whole document, choose **Select All** from the **Edit** menu or press **CTRL+A**.
2. Choose **Paragraph** from the **Format** menu.
3. Click on the **Indents and Spacing** tab, then select a line spacing setting from the **Line spacing** list. See Figure 24.
4. Click **OK**.

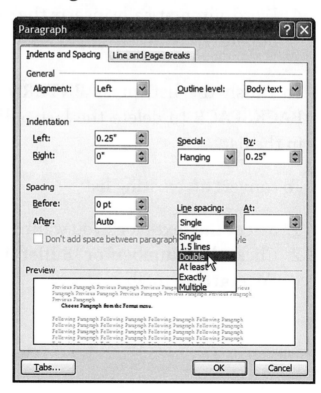

Figure 24: Paragraph formatting dialog box

How To Make A Bulleted List

Bulleted and numbered lists are often used in documents. With Word, you can create bulleted or numbered lists as you type or convert existing text into either of them. Here is how to create one as you type.

1. Type **1.** to start a numbered list, or * (asterisk) to start a bulleted list, and then press **SPACEBAR** or **TAB**.
2. Type any text you want.
3. Press **ENTER** to add the next list item.
4. Word automatically inserts the next number or bullet.

To finish the list, press **ENTER** twice, or press **BACKSPACE** to delete the last bullet or number in the list.

To convert an existing list:

1. Select the text block you want to convert.
2. Click the **Number or Bullet** icon from the **Formatting** toolbar.

How To Format A Bullet Or Numbered List

You can use other characters or number styles in your lists.

Here's how to change them for an existing list:

1. Click **Format**.
2. Click **Bullets and numbering**.
3. Click either the **Bullets** tab or the **Numbered** tab depending upon what you want to format.
4. Choose a formatting style as shown in Figure 25.
5. Click **OK**.

The format option you change will be used for all bullet and number lists.

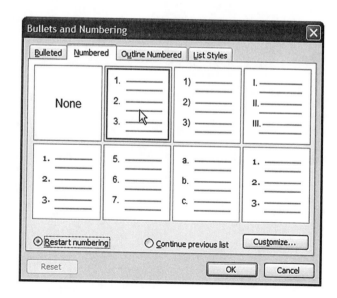

Figure 25: Formatting bullets and numbering

How To Add Page Numbers To A Document

If you need to add page numbers to your document or brochure, follow these steps:

1. Choose **Page Numbers** from the **Insert** menu.
2. In the dialog box, select the **Position and Alignment** for your page numbers.
3. The **Format** button allows you to choose different number formats, as well as control the page numbers in documents with multiple sections.

How To Delete Page Numbers

If you need to remove the page numbers from a document, follow these steps:

1. Choose **Header and Footer** from the **View** menu.
2. Using your mouse, select the frame around the page number (it is similar to a graphic element).
3. Press the **DELETE** or **BACKSPACE** key to delete the page numbers throughout the document.

How To Remove Page Numbers
From The First Page

You may not want the page number to show on a title page, or the first page, of a document. Here is how to remove it:

1. Choose **Page Numbers** from the **Insert** menu.
2. Clear the **Show Numbers on First Page** check box.
3. Click **OK**.

How To Insert Or Delete Page Breaks

When you get to the bottom of a page, Word will automatically insert a page break for you. But sometimes you may want to control where the page break occurs. Follow these steps to insert a page break where you want it:

1. Place the cursor on the line where you want to insert a page break.
2. Click the **Insert** menu and **Choose Break**.
3. Select the **Page Break** radio button. You can also insert a page break by pressing **CTRL+ENTER**.
4. Click **OK**.

To delete a page break:

1. Switch to **Normal** view (Normal on the View menu). Page breaks are identified on your document as dotted lines (page breaks you insert are identified as "Page Break".
2. Click at the left edge of the screen to select the page break.
3. Press the Delete key or click on the **Cut** button. You can also click below the page break, then press **Backspace**.

How To Keep Paragraphs On The Same Page

Often Word will insert a page break in the middle of a paragraph. If you want to keep the paragraphs together on the same page:

1. Select the paragraph, then choose **Paragraph** from the **Format** menu.
2. Click on the **Lines and Page Breaks** tab.
3. Check the **Keep lines together** check box.
4. Click **OK**.

How To Indent Paragraphs

Word by default left justifies a paragraph. You can indent it differently by following these steps.

1. Choose **Paragraph** from the **Format** menu.
2. Set **Left** and **Right** under **Indentation**.

Another way is to use the Ruler. You should see three symbols that look like an hourglass sitting on a box on the ruler's left side. Moving these symbols anywhere on the ruler affects the current paragraph or selection as follows:

1. Moving the top triangle indents the first line of the paragraph (or the first line in every paragraph you have selected).
2. Moving the bottom triangle indents all lines in the current paragraph (or all lines in all paragraphs you have selected) except the first line.
3. Moving the square moves the "hourglass" and sets a normal indent (all lines in the current paragraph or selection will be left aligned).

How To Create A Table

Tables are used to present and summarize data in a document. Here are the basics of creating a table in Word:

1. Choose **Insert** from the **Table** menu.
2. Select **Table** to display the **Insert Table** dialog box.
3. Set the number of columns and rows under **Table Size**. See Figure 26.

After you create your table, use the other options on the **Table** menu to change its appearance.

There is also an **Insert Table** button on the **Standard** toolbar that allows you to create a table by clicking and dragging through a grid to specify the number of rows and columns for the table.

How To Create A Table, Cont.

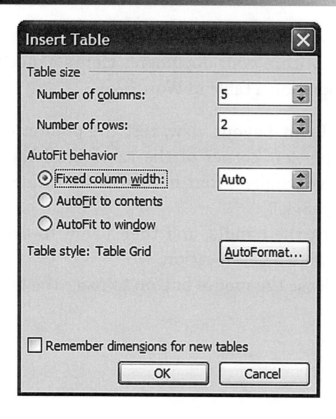

Figure 26: Insert table dialog box

Adjust The Table Placement In Word

Once you create a table, you may want to reposition it within your document. Here's a quick way to reposition a table in Word.

1. In **Print Layout** view, rest the pointer on the upper-left corner of the table until the table move handle (a four-headed arrow inside a box) appears.
2. Click the handle, and then use it to drag the table to a new location.
3. Release the mouse button to place the table.

How To Make Larger Toolbar Icons

You can make the toolbar icons appear larger in Word. This makes them easier to see and click. Here's how:

1. Choose **Tools**, then **Customize**.
2. When the **Customize** multi-tabbed dialog box appears, choose **Options**.
3. Select the **Large icons** check box. See Figure 27.
4. You should now see large icons. Click **OK** if you like it, click **Cancel** to change the icons back to their original size.

Figure 27: Enabling large icons in Word

How To Put A Digital Picture In A Document

To insert an image file into your document:

1. From the **Insert** menu, choose **Picture**.
2. Choose **File**, locate the file, then click **Insert**.

Another method is to simply copy a picture you have open in a graphics application or from Explorer, then paste it into your Word document.

How To Use Word To Make A Web Page

You can use Word as an easy way to create Web pages. It has a **Save as Web Page** command on the **File** menu.

In addition, there is an **Insert Hyperlink** button on the **Standard** toolbar, plus two additional toolbars for the Web: **Web** and **Web Tools**. To activate these toolbars click **Toolbars** then choose the **View** menu.

If you save a Word document as a Web page, Word includes XML (eXtensible Markup Language) tags, which enhances the format of the Web page, but may cause problems with some Web browsers. As you might expect, pages created with Microsoft Word work best with Microsoft Internet Explorer.

How To Remove All Document Formatting

Here's a method to easily remove all of the formatting from a Word document or just a selected portion of the document:

1. Select the whole document by pressing **CTRL+A** or just select the portion of the document you wish to change.
2. Press **CTRL+SHIFT+N**.

All of your formatting is removed from the document or selection.

How To Display The Status Bar

The Status Bar, located at the bottom of the Word workspace, provides a lot of useful information. For example, you can find out what line number you are on, column, page number, and a lot more.

If you don't see the Status Bar, here is how to turn it on:

1. Click **Tools**.
2. Click **Options**.
3. Click the **View** tab.
4. Click the **Status bar** check box under **Show**.
5. Click **OK**.

You should see the Status bar at the bottom of your Word workspace.

How To Use Status Bar Shortcuts

Did you know that the status bar, that area at the bottom of Word documents where the page number appears, also provides shortcuts to a number of very useful features? Here are a few you may want to use:

1. To open the **Find and Replace** dialog box, double-click any location indicator on the status bar, such as the page number or section number.
2. To turn the macro recorder on or off, double-click **REC**.
3. To turn the Track Changes feature on or off, double-click **TRK**.
4. To turn extend selection mode on or off, double-click **EXT**.
5. To turn overtype mode on or off, double-click **OVR**.
6. To change the language format of selected text, double-click **Language**.
7. To resolve errors in grammar or spelling, double-click the **Spelling and Grammar Status** icon.

When the features on the Status bar are turned off, their labels appear dimmed.

The Senior's Guide to Computer Tips & Tricks

How To Quickly Access Documents You Use Most Often

The Work menu is a great Word feature that few people know about. You can use the Work menu to keep an easily accessible list of your favorite Word files.

To add the **Work** menu to the menu bar or a toolbar:

1. On the **Tools** menu, click **Customize**, and then click the **Commands** tab.
2. In the **Categories** box, click **Built-in Menus**.
3. Click **Work** in the **Commands** box and drag it to the menu bar or displayed toolbar.

With the **Work** menu in place, you can add any open Word document to your list. Here are the options:

- To add the current document to the **Work** menu, on the **Work** menu, click **Add to Work Menu**.
- To open a document on the **Work** menu, on the **Work** menu, click the document you want to open.

To remove a document from the Work menu:

1. Press **CTRL+ALT+-** (dash key). Your cursor will look like a large, bold underscore.
2. On the **Work** menu, click the document you want to remove.

Ten Essential Shortcuts For Word

The following list contains ten must-know keyboard shortcuts for Word:

1. **CTRL+C** to copy selected text or object.
2. **CTRL+V** to paste.
3. **ALT+F+S** to save a file.
4. **F7** to spell check.
5. **SHIFT+F7** to open the thesaurus.
6. **F1** to display the help system.
7. **CTRL+Z** to undo the last command.
8. Double-click the ruler margin to open the **Page Setup** dialog box.
9. Double-click an indent marker to open the **Paragraph** dialog box.
10. Double-click a tab stop to open the **Tabs** dialog box.

How To Count The Words In Your Document

Counting words in a document couldn't be easier. You might be amazed at how many words are in any size document. Here's how to count your words:

1. Click **Tools**.
2. Click **Word Count**. Word displays a dialog box with the word count along with a number of other statistics like pages and paragraphs.

If you want to display the **Word Count** toolbar, click **Show Toolbar**.

How To Increase The List Of Recently Used Documents

In the File menu Word displays a list of the last four documents you opened. You may find that showing four is not enough. You can configure Word to show up to nine recently opened documents.

To increase the number of documents displayed on the recently used documents list:

1. On the **Tools** menu, click **Options**, and then click the **General** tab.
2. In the **Recently used file list box**, specify the number of recently used files that you want to appear in the **File** menu.
3. Click **OK**.

How To E-mail A Document From Word

Open or create the document you want to send in Word and do the following:

1. Click on the **E-Mail** button on the toolbar while in Word.
2. Word will then display an e-mail header at the top of the document.
3. Fill in the appropriate address and subject fields.
4. Click the **Send a Copy** button.

Word places the e-mail in the outgoing folder of your e-mail program. To actually send the e-mail, you need to go to the e-mail program and send as you normally would.

PART 4

Microsoft Outlook

In a nutshell, Outlook is a powerful personal information and e-mail tool. With one application, you can manage your address book, keep detailed information on contacts, manage your calendar and so much more!

Outlook is bundled with the Office productivity suite. If you have Word chances are you have Outlook.

Windows XP ships with a scaled down version of Outlook called Outlook Express. This part of our book focuses on Outlook, not Outlook Express. However, many of the tips will work with it as well.

Using Folders To Organize Your Inbox

If you get a lot of e-mail from different people or groups, try using folders to organize them. You can also create subfolders under those folders to further organize your messages. You can use one of the following methods to create folders:

Method 1:

1. Click **File** then choose **Folder** then **New Folder**.
2. In the **Create New Folder** dialog box, enter the name you want for the new folder. See Figure 28 on the next page.
3. Make sure the **Folder Contains** box shows in the **Mail and Post Items**.
4. Select your **Mailbox** at the top of the **Folder List** to create a folder or an existing folder in your **Mailbox** to create a subfolder. Select a folder by single clicking it. Figure 28 shows the **Inbox** selected.
5. Click **OK**.

Using Folders To Organize Your Inbox, Cont.

Method 2:

1. Right-click on your **Mailbox** at the top of the **Folder List** for a folder or one of the folders in your **Mailbox** to create a subfolder under it.
2. Select **New Folder** from the shortcut list.
3. Follow steps 3, 4, and 5 from Method 1 to complete.

Figure 28: Create new mail folder dialog box

How To Move E-mail Between Folders

Tired of moving one message at a time to another folder or subfolder? Here are two methods to move multiple e-mails at once:

Method 1:

1. Click on the first message.
2. Hold down the **SHIFT** key and click on the last message.
3. Drag the entire group of messages to another folder or subfolder.

Method 2:

1. Click on the first message.
2. Hold down the **CTRL** key and click on each additional message (while continuing to hold the **CTRL** key down) until all the messages are selected.
3. Drag all the highlighted messages at the same time by dragging from anyone of them to another folder or subfolder.

How To Sort E-mail

Did you know that you can sort e-mail by date received, sender, attachments, or subject? This is a very powerful tool and is very easy to use.

Simply click on the column header of the option that best fits your need. Clicking once puts them in ascending order. Clicking again puts them in descending order.

The default listing is in chronological order of date received.

How To Color-Code Your E-mail

Color coding messages makes it easy to identify e-mails from particular people or groups. For example, you might make e-mails from your children green while those from your best friend blue.

Here are the steps on how to do this:

1. Select a message in your Inbox that you want to color code.
2. Click **Tools** then choose **Organize** then **Using Colors**.
3. Select the desired color.
4. Click **Apply** Color.
5. Click the **X** in the upper right-hand corner of the **Organize** dialog box to close.

How To Enable Read Receipt

Outlook's Read Receipt feature sends you an e-mail receipt when the recipient reads your e-mail. It is analogous to registered mail. To use this feature, do the following:

1. Compose or reply to an e-mail as usual.
2. Click the **Options** button.
3. Place a checkmark in the box for **Request a read receipt for this message**. See Figure 29 below.
4. Click **Close** to close the Options dialog box.

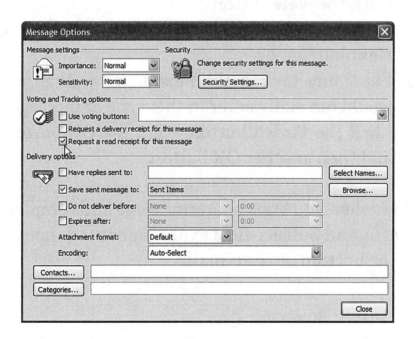

Figure 29: Enabling a read receipt

How To Use Automatic Signatures

Do you always sign your e-mail messages the same way? Or do you send messages that require different signatures? Either way, you can eliminate some typing by saving one or more of your signatures.

Here is how:

1. Select **Tools**, choose **Options**.
2. Click the **Mail Format** tab and then the **Signatures** button.
3. Click the **New** button.
4. Enter the name for the signature and click the **Next** button.
5. Enter any text in the next window that you would normally enter in this type of message.
6. Click the **Finish** button, then the **OK** button, and then another **OK** button.

Now when you start a new message and complete the To and Subject fields your signature appears at the bottom of the e-mail.

How To Edit The Subject Line

Have you noticed that the subject lines of messages sent to you don't always express what's in the message? To change the subject to make it more meaningful:

1. Open a message by double clicking on it.
2. Either place your cursor in the subject text area or select all or part of the subject text with your mouse.
3. Edit the text as you would edit any text in a Word document.
4. Close the message.
5. Click **Yes** when it asks if you want to save the changes.

How To Add An Attachment To An E-mail

Did you know that you can attach a file to an e-mail and send it to someone? You can send almost any type of file; Word document, spreadsheet, or digital picture for example.

Here is how to add an attachment:

1. Click the **New** button to create a new message as normal.
2. Click inside the body of the item, and then click **Insert** on the menu then choose **File**, or click the **Paperclip** on the toolbar.
3. Select the file that you want to attach, and then click **Insert**.
4. Finish typing your message.
5. Click **Send** to start the message on its way.

The e-mail might take a few minutes to send depending on the size of the attachment. It is also courteous not to send too big of an attachment to someone without notifying them. The recipient may have size restrictions on their e-mail account. A large attachment, therefore, may fill up their inbox.

How To Open An Attachment

If someone sends you an attachment, follow these instructions to open it:

1. Double-click the e-mail with the attachment. The e-mail should have a small paperclip associated with it.
2. Under the subject line, you should see the attachment. Double-click the attachment to open it. Outlook will find the correct program to open the file.

Warning! Virus and spyware hackers use e-mail attachments to attack your computer. Do not open attachments from people you do not know, and always use an anti-virus program that scans attachments prior to opening it.

How To Save An Attachment

Instead of opening the attachment, you can save it to your hard drive for future use. Here are the steps to save an attachment:

1. Open or view the message that has an attachment.
2. Right-click the attachment and select **Save As** from the shortcut menu.
3. Select the location for the file and click the **Save** button.

To save room in your Inbox, consider deleting the e-mail with the attachment. The attachment is safe on your hard drive if you have saved it as described above. It may not hurt to open and verify the file before deleting it.

How To Save Multiple Attachments

If an e-mail contains multiple attachments, you can save all of them with a few keystrokes. Here's the method:

1. Open the message that contains the file attachments you want to save.
2. Hold down **SHIFT**, and then click each attachment so that they are all selected.
3. On the **File** menu, click **Save Attachments**.

How To Create An E-mail Shortcut

Why not create shortcuts for your favorite e-mail recipients? This allows you to send an e-mail to someone with a simple double click.

You can do this easily:

1. Right click a blank space on your desktop and select **New** then choose **Shortcut** from the shortcut menu.
2. In the **Command Line** enter **mailto:** and then an e-mail address. For example, Figure 30 shows an e-mail shortcut being made to Rebecca. The entry is: mailto:rebecca@theseniorsguide.com.
3. Give the shortcut a name so that you will know what it is (ex., E-mail to Rebecca).

When you double-click the shortcut Outlook will automatically complete the To field with that person's e-mail address. All you have to do is fill in the subject line and body text.

How To Create An E-mail Shortcut, Cont.

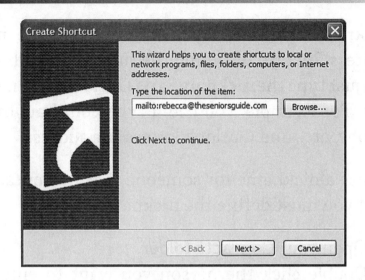

Figure 30: Create an e-mail shortcut

How To Use E-mail Nicknames

Nicknames make it easy to enter someone's e-mail address. Instead of typing the full e-mail address, you just type the nickname and Outlook fills in the rest. For example, you could type Son, Daughter, Hubby, etc., and Outlook knows the address.

To use a nickname for someone in your Contacts, first you must define the nickname:

1. Open your **Contacts** folder.
2. Double click the person you want to enter a nickname for or create a new Contact for that person.
3. While in the **Contact Info** window, select the **Details** tab, and complete the **Nickname** field. See Figure 31 on the next page
4. Click **OK**.

When addressing an e-mail to that person just type the nickname in the To, CC, or BCC field and Outlook will fill in the rest when you move your cursor to the next field.

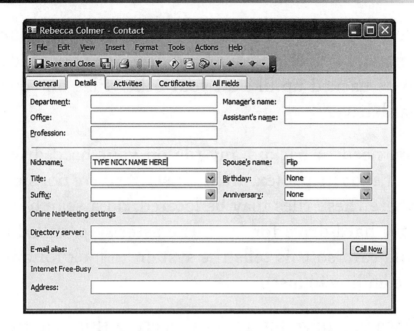

Figure 31: Create e-mail nickname dialog box

How To Back Up Your Personal
E-mail Folder

Outlook stores e-mails and contacts in your Personal Folder on your hard drive, so this needs to be backed up like all your other files on your hard drive.

You need to backup any file on your hard drive that ends in .pst (ex. archive.pst). If you're not sure where these files may be located, do a search on your hard drive for *.pst (the asterisk is called a wild card so this tells the system to look for any file ending in .pst).

Once you have found files meeting this criteria, be sure they are added in your regular backup routine. You'll be glad you did if your hard drive crashes.

How To Send An E-mail At A Specified Time

Outlook can send a message at a later date or time on your behalf. Here is how to set up a timed message:

1. Open or compose a new message.
2. Click the **Options** button (or select **View** then choose **Options**).
3. Select **Do Not Deliver Before** and then click the down arrow and select the date you wish the message sent. See Figure 32.
4. Choose the time and date to send the e-mail.
5. Click **Close** and Outlook will send it on that day.

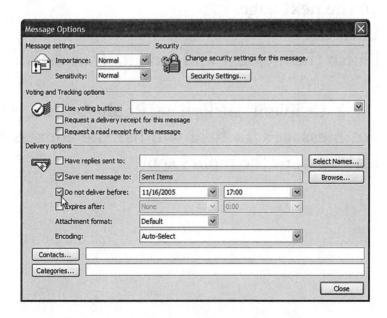

Figure 32: Delayed e-mail delivery

How To Send Message Replies
To Someone Else

Want to send a message to several recipients but need them to reply back to another person? This is helpful if you are e-mailing invitations and want the RSVP to go to a coordinator. If so, do the following:

1. Compose your message as usual but before sending it click the **Options** button.
2. Under the **Delivery** options, select **Have Replies Sent To:**.
3. Type in the e-mail address of the person to which the replies should be sent. See Figure 33 on the next page.
4. Click **OK** .
5. Finish the message and send it off as usual.

When a recipient clicks the **Reply** button, the return message's **To** field will list the address to which you want the replies sent.

How To Send Message Replies
To Someone Else, Cont.

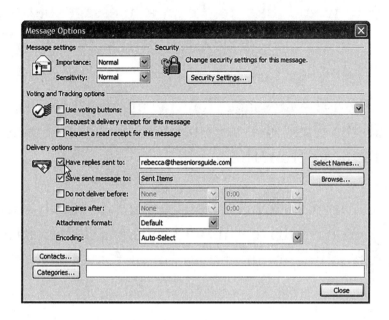

Figure 33: Configuring a reply-to address

Save The Message But Not The Attachment

If you would like to keep a message but not the attachment, simply remove it by doing the following:

1. Open the message that has an attachment.
2. Right-click the attachment listed and select **Remove** from the menu.

If you are concerned about using too much space on your hard drive, this will save a little by getting the attachment out of your Inbox folder.

Disable Word As Your Default E-mail Editor

If you have both Microsoft Word and Outlook installed, Outlook will try to use Word as its default e-mail editor. This isn't bad because Word has lots of editing features that you can use to spruce up your e-mails. However, it may be more than what you need and it consumes a lot of computer resources.

Try switching to Outlook's default editor if you find Word too confusing or slow.

Here's how:

1. On the **Tools** menu, click **Options**, and then click the **Mail Format** tab.
2. Click to select or click to clear the **Use Microsoft Word to edit e-mail messages** check box.

How To Recall An E-mail

Ever sent an e-mail you wish you hadn't? Try these steps to recall the message:

1. Open your **Sent Items** folder.
2. Double-click the message you want to recall.
3. Select **Actions** then **Recall This Message**.
4. Select "**Delete unread copies of this message.**"
5. If you want to receive notification about the success of the recall, select "**Tell me if recall succeeds or fails for each recipient.**"

Recalling a message doesn't always work. Here are several reasons why it doesn't:

- The recipient uses an e-mail client other than Outlook.
- The recipient does not have Outlook open.
- The message has already been moved from the recipient's Inbox.
- The message has already been read or viewed by the recipient.

How To Use Blind Carbon-Copy

The Blind Carbon-Copy (Bcc) field lets you send a copy of a message with that person's e-mail address hidden from all other recipients. In a normal carbon-copied (Cc) message, everyone sees everyone else's address.

Outlook doesn't always display the Bcc field. Making it visible depends upon whether or not Word is used for editing e-mails.

Word editor:

1. Start composing a new e-mail.
2. Click on the down arrow to the right of the **Options** button and select **Bcc**.

Outlook editor:

1. Start composing a new e-mail.
2. Select **View** then choose **Bcc**.

Now the Bcc field will show up on all your e-mails. You can turn it off by reversing the above steps.

Find Very Large Messages In Outlook

E-mail can slowly grow and take up a lot of space on your hard drive. You may recover some space by deleting larger messages, which generally have attachments.

Fortunately, Outlook lets you search for these very large messages. Here's how:

1. Click **Tools** then choose **Advanced Find**, then the **More Choices** tab.
2. Click **Messages** in the **Look For** box.
3. In the **Size** list, click **Greater Than**, and then enter a number such as **500**. The size is in kilobytes, so this equals 500 KB.
4. Select any remaining search options you want and click **Find Now**.

You can delete the messages out of the list to save space. If you need to save even more space, you can repeat the process, but enter a smaller number such as 250 to find the next smaller items, and so on.

Make A New Contact Out Of An E-mail

When you get an e-mail from someone special, you may want to save their e-mail address in the contact list. Here is an easy way to save the address:

1. Open the e-mail.
2. Right click on the e-mail address of the sender.
3. Click on **Add to Contacts**.
4. Fill out the contact information form with the appropriate information.
5. Click **Save** and close from the toolbar.

How To Find Related Messages

You can quickly and easily find and display messages about a related topic. This is useful to gather all the messages in a specific e-mail thread.

Here's how:

1. Open an e-mail about the topic.
2. Click the **Actions** menu, then choose **Find All**, then **Related Messages**.

How To Forward An E-mail

Have you ever gotten an e-mail that you wanted to share with someone else? Here's how you can easily forward it:

1. Right-click the e-mail you want to forward.
2. Select **Forward** from the shortcut menu. You could also open the e-mail and choose **Forward** from the toolbar.
3. A new message will be created with the original message included in the e-mail body.
4. Address the message to the person you wish to forward it to and...
5. Add any additional information you want to.
6. Click **Send**.

Keep in mind that not everything you find funny, helpful or informative will be appreciated by everyone in your address book. Be selective in what you forward.

How To Add Holidays To The Calendar

Here's how you can add the typical holidays like Easter, Memorial Day, Labor Day, Thanksgiving, and Christmas to your calendar:

1. Click on **Calendar** in your **Folder List**.
2. Click **Tools** > **Options** > **Calendar Options**.
3. Click the **Add Holidays** button.
4. Click the check box next to the holiday set you would like to include in your calendar.
5. Click **OK**, then wait a few seconds and click **OK** twice more to close all open dialog boxes.
6. Check your calendar for holiday markings.

Counting Messages In A Folder

Outlook can show you the total number of messages in a folder using green brackets "[]", or it displays the unread message count in blue parenthesis "()". This feature provides a visual clue as to how full your Inbox is.

Here's how to enable this feature:

1. Right click on the folder in the folder list.
2. Choose **Properties**.
3. Choose either "Show number of unread items" or "Show total number of items."
4. Click **OK**.

You should now see a number in either brackets or parenthesis. If you choose to view the number of unread items, you may not see a number if you do not have an unread message.

How To Resend An E-mail

Do you need to resend a message? You might if you forgot to add an attachment or mistyped the person's e-mail address. Fortunately you don't have to retype the entire e-mail, Outlook has a way to quickly resend the same message.

Here's how:

1. Click on the **Sent Items** folder to view a list of sent e-mails.
2. Open the e-mail you want to resend by double-clicking it.
3. Click the **Actions** menu and choose **Resend Message**.
4. You can now correct any mistakes like changing the recipient, editing the text, or adding an attachment.

KEYBOARD SHORTCUTS

WINDOWS XP	
CTRL+C	Copy selected text or item
CTRL+X	Cut selected text or item
CTRL+V	Paste
CTRL+Z	Undo
SHIFT+DELETE	Delete the selected item permanently without placing the item in the Recycle Bin
CTRL while dragging an item	Copy the selected item
CTRL+SHIFT while dragging an item	Create a shortcut to the selected item
F2 key	Rename the selected item
CTRL+SHIFT with any of the arrow keys	Highlight a block of text
SHIFT with any of the arrow keys	Select more than one item in a window or on the desktop, or select text in a document
CTRL+A	Select all
F3 key	Search for a file or a folder
ALT+ENTER	View the properties for the selected item
ALT+F4	Close the active item, or quit the active program
ALT+ENTER	Display the properties of the selected object

KEYBOARD SHORTCUTS

WINDOWS XP	
ALT+SPACEBAR	Open the shortcut menu for the active window
CTRL+F4	Close the active document in programs that enable you to have multiple documents open simultaneously
ALT+TAB	Switch between the open items
ALT+ESC	Cycle through items in the order that they had been opened
F6 key	Cycle through the screen elements in a window or on the desktop
F4 key	Display the Address bar list in My Computer or Windows Explorer
SHIFT+F10	Display the shortcut menu for the selected item
ALT+SPACEBAR	Display the System menu for the active window
CTRL+ESC	Display the Start menu
ALT+Underlined letter in a menu name	Display the corresponding menu
F10 key	Activate the menu bar in the active program
F5 key	Update the active window
ESC	Cancel the current task

KEYBOARD SHORTCUTS

WORD 2000, WORD 2003, WORD XP	
CTRL+C	Copy selected text or object
CTRL+X	Cut selected text or object
CTRL+V	Paste
CTRL+Z	Undo your last action
CTRL+A	Select all the text within your document
CTRL+B	Bold text
CTRL+I	Italicize text
CTRL+U	Underline
CTRL+SHIFT+<	Decrease font size
CTRL+SHIFT+>	Increase font size
CTRL+ENTER	Create page break
CTRL+N	Create new document
CTRL+O	Open My Documents window
CTRL+W	Close a document
CTRL+S	Save a document
CTRL+P	Print a document
ALT+CTRL+I	Preview what you're about to print

KEYBOARD SHORTCUTS

OUTLOOK	
E-MAIL	
CTRL+SHIFT+I	Switch to Inbox
CTRL+SHIFT+O	Switch to Outbox
CTRL+SHIFT+B	Switch to the Address Book
CTRL+R	Reply to a message
CTRL+SHIFT+R	Reply to all
CTRL+M or F5	Check for new e-mail
CTRL+Q	Mark a message as read
CALENDAR	
ALT+C	Accept
ALT+D	Decline
ALT+Hyphen	Switch to weeks
ALT+Number	Display x number of days (1-10)
ALT+Equals	Switch to months
CTRL+Tab or F6	Move between Calendar, Tasks, and Folders
Left Arrow	Previous day
Right Arrow	Next day
ALT+Down arrow	Go to the same day in the next week
ALT+Up arrow	Go to the same day in the previous week

KEYBOARD SHORTCUTS

OUTLOOK OTHERS	
F11	Open the find a contact box
CTRL+SHIFT+K	Open a new task
CTRL+SHIFT+Q	Open a new meeting request
CTRL+SHIFT+C	Open a new contact
CTRL+SHIFT+M	Open a new e-mail message

INDEX

INDEX